WITHDRAWN

Troubled Treasures: World Heritage Sites

GALÁPAGOS ISLANDS

Cynthia Kennedy Henzel

ABDO Publishing Company

visit us at
www.abdopublishing.com

Published by ABDO Publishing Company, 8000 West 78th Street, Edina, Minnesota 55439.
Copyright © 2011 by Abdo Consulting Group, Inc. International copyrights reserved in all
countries. No part of this book may be reproduced in any form without written permission from the
publisher. The Checkerboard Library™ is a trademark and logo of ABDO Publishing Company.

Printed in the United States of America, North Mankato, Minnesota.
102010
012011

 PRINTED ON RECYCLED PAPER

Cover Photo: Getty Images
Interior Photos: Alamy p. 25; Corbis pp. 21, 26; Getty Images pp. 17, 19, 20, 27;
 iStockphoto pp. 1, 4, 5, 15; Mark Moffett / Minden Pictures p. 15; Peter Arnold p. 29;
 Photolibrary pp. 13, 18; Tui De Roy / Minden Pictures pp. 8–9, 15;
 Tui De Roy / Minden Pictures / National Geographic Stock p. 23

Series Coordinator: BreAnn Rumsch
Editors: Heidi M.D. Elston, BreAnn Rumsch
Art Direction & Cover Design: Neil Klinepier

Library of Congress Cataloging-in-Publication Data

Henzel, Cynthia Kennedy, 1954-
 Galápagos Islands / Cynthia Kennedy Henzel.
  p. cm. -- (Troubled treasures : world heritage sites)
 Includes index.
 ISBN 978-1-61613-563-8
 1. Galapagos Islands--Juvenile literature. I. Title.
 F3741.G2H46 2011
 986.6'5--dc22
        2010021311

CONTENTS

The Galápagos Islands are a famous, exciting place. Pirates, whalers, and scientists have all been amazed by the wonders there. Today, visitors are still wowed.

The islands lie in the Pacific Ocean. They are located on the **equator** about 600 miles (1,000 km) west of Ecuador. This South American country governs the islands.

There are 13 major and 6 smaller islands in the Galápagos. More than 100 tiny islands and rocks also rise above the waves.

The Galápagos cover 23,000 square miles (59,500 sq km). However, just 3,093 square miles (8,010 sq km) of this area is land. The ocean around the islands makes up the remaining area.

NORTH AMERICA

Galápagos Islands

EQUATOR

SOUTH AMERICA

Pacific Ocean

N

The Galápagos Islands offer visitors many amazing sights to see!

Many rare plants and animals live in the Galápagos. They help scientists learn about life on Earth. **UNESCO** officials recognized the importance of the Galápagos Islands by naming them a World Heritage site. This will help preserve the natural wonders there for years to come.

The Galápagos Islands have been forming for millions of years. Some are still growing! The islands are actually a group of volcanoes. They formed over a hot spot. A hot spot is a fixed location near Earth's surface.

At the hot spot, melted rock called magma rises from within Earth. Over many years, this forms a volcano.

Eventually, the volcano grows tall enough to rise above the water. Then, it becomes an island.

The Galápagos Islands sit on a

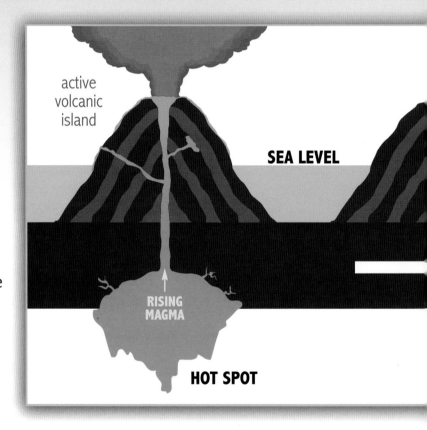

active volcanic island

SEA LEVEL

RISING MAGMA

HOT SPOT

tectonic plate called the Nazca Plate. Tectonic plates are pieces of Earth's outer shell. They move several inches each year. That's slow! But over millions of years, that adds up to many miles.

As the Nazca Plate moves, the volcano slowly moves away from its magma source. Once it has separated, the island stops growing. It then begins to erode. Volcanic rock slowly turns to soil and washes into the sea. In time, the island sinks beneath the waves.

Meanwhile, a new volcano has begun forming over the hot spot. Eventually, there are several islands. Together, they form an **archipelago**.

separated volcanic island

eroding volcanic island

MOVING PLATE

The Nazca Plate is like a conveyor belt. As it moves across the hot spot, it takes the old volcano with it.

The most recent eruptions have occurred on the island of Isabela.

The Nazca Plate moves toward the southeast. So, the oldest islands are in the southeast part of the **archipelago**.

Española is the oldest island. Some scientists estimate it is 3 to 5 million years old. Underwater mountains rest nearby. These were islands long before today's islands formed.

The middle-aged islands sit in the middle of the group. These have soil and support life.

In the northwest, Fernandina is the youngest island. It is about 700,000 years old. Beyond it, new islands are slowly forming underwater.

Some of the Galápagos Islands still have active volcanoes. More than 60 eruptions have occurred in the last 200 years! Today, most volcanic activity occurs on the islands of Isabela and Fernandina.

More to Explore
Isabela is the largest island in the Galápagos. It makes up more than half the total land area!

The Galápagos Islands rest in an interesting spot. Due to their location, several ocean currents travel near them. These affect weather and life on the islands.

From December to May, the Panama Current carries warm water south. Then, the water joins the South **Equatorial** Current. This current travels west. It makes the islands warm and rainy.

From June to November, the Humboldt Current brings cold water north. This makes the islands cooler and dryer than many areas along the equator.

GALÁPAGOS ISLANDS WORLD HERITAGE AREA

Pinta
Wolf
Genovesa
Marchena
Santiago
Bartolomé
Seymour
Rábida
Baltra
Fernandina
Santa Cruz
Santa Fé
Pinzón
San Cristóbal
Isabela
Floreana
Española

N
W   E
S

Detail Area

IMPORTANT CURRENTS

Panama Current

South Equatorial Current

Cromwell Current

Galápagos Islands

ECUADOR

Humboldt Current

SOUTH AMERICA

Pacific Ocean

The Cromwell Current runs east. It travels deep underwater along the **equator**. Near the Galápagos, its cold water surfaces. This brings food from under the sea. Many animals depend on this food to survive.

Sometimes, the cold water does not rise. About every seven years, a weather event called El Niño takes place. During this time, warmer northern currents shift south. This increases rainfall and the ocean's temperature. It also stops cold water from bringing food up to Galápagos creatures.

Tomás de Berlanga discovered the Galápagos Islands in 1535. He named them Las Encantados, which means "The Enchanted." That is because they were difficult to find.

Yet, this made the islands ideal for pirates! In 1683, British pirate Ambrose Cowley first mapped the area. Then in 1709, British pirate William Dampier arrived. He hid stolen treasure on the islands. Dampier also wrote about the strange plants and animals there.

By the late 1700s, whalers began replacing the pirates. British captain James Colnett and his men hunted whales for whale oil. Whalers continued this practice until the 1860s.

Humans **exploited** other animals in the Galápagos, too. They hunted sea lions for fur. And, they captured giant tortoises for food.

The tortoises could be kept alive on a ship for months without food or water. So, sailors always had a steady supply of fresh meat. They killed as many as 200,000 tortoises.

More to Explore
The Galápagos are named for their tortoise residents. In fact, the Spanish word for "tortoise" is *galápago*.

Before humans arrived, 14 tortoise species called the islands home. Today, just 11 survive.

EVOLUTION REVOLUTION

Meanwhile, scientists began to show interest in the Galápagos Islands. Naturalist Charles Darwin became one of the first to visit the area.

In 1831, Darwin set sail on a journey around the world. His job was to collect new plants and animals. For five years, Darwin collected thousands of examples.

Darwin spent just a few weeks in the Galápagos Islands. But, the things he saw altered ideas in science and religion forever. At the time, most people believed the world didn't change. Yet, Darwin saw volcanoes and earthquakes change the islands.

In addition, Darwin saw many new animals. Birds called finches lived on the islands. He noted many beak shapes among them.

Darwin believed each bird's beak was suited to its own diet and **environment**. He wondered if the birds had changed from one type into several species. But how had this happened?

Cactus finch

Ground finch

Tree finch

Fit for a Feast

The Galápagos finches showed Darwin how animals could adapt to different conditions. For example, cactus finches have beaks shaped for eating from cactus plants. Ground finches have short, thick beaks. These help them eat seeds from the ground. Tree finches eat insects with their thin, sharp beaks.

For more than 20 years, Darwin thought about what he had seen. Eventually, he had a theory. He called it evolution. This is a process of change over time.

Darwin believed that the Galápagos finches had evolved from one earlier species. He believed this happened because the birds were separated on the different islands.

In addition, Darwin believed in a process called natural selection. He noted that the living beings best suited to their **environment** produce more young. So, favorable qualities pass on. Meanwhile, unfavorable features end.

Darwin's theories suggest that a species can change over time. This explains how and why the Galápagos finches have different beaks.

Darwin's ideas challenged many people's beliefs. So, he hesitated to make them public. But in 1859, he finally published his theories in a book. *On the Origin of Species* began an argument among scientists, religious leaders, and others. This discussion about how life began continues today.

More to Explore
Darwin's finches are found throughout the Galápagos Islands. The 13 species live nowhere else in the world.

Charles Darwin

Numerous plant and animal species in the Galápagos are endemic. That means they exist only in one place and nowhere else.

For example, the opuntia cactus is found in dryer areas of the islands. This cactus's pads offer shade and food to some reptiles. Several types of birds nest among the pads and the trunks. Some feed on the flower nectar.

The most famous animals there are the Galápagos giant tortoises. They live on about six of the islands. Some can grow up to six feet (2 m) long. And, they can weigh nearly 700 pounds (300 kg)!

The Galápagos Islands are home to many other reptiles.

Galápagos land iguana

The Galápagos land iguana dwells on several islands. Sadly, their numbers are at risk.

Marine iguanas are also found around the islands. They dive into the cold sea to feed on algae. Then, they warm up in the sun.

Galápagos sea lions are also famous. They live on most of the islands. Their colonies can be found on sandy beaches and rocky island shores.

The marine iguana is the world's only seagoing lizard

*The flightless cormorant is one of
the rarest bird species in the world.*

In addition to Darwin's finches, several other endemic birds live in the Galápagos. The flightless cormorant's wings have adapted for swimming. They became shorter! Now, this bird can no longer fly. Instead, it swims underwater to snatch fish.

One of the world's smallest penguin species is the Galápagos penguin. This flightless bird stands just 14 inches (35 cm) tall. It is the only **endangered** penguin species.

The blue-footed boobie is native to the Galápagos. This striking seabird dives deep into the ocean for a meal. It nests in colonies on open ground.

Meanwhile, the red-footed boobie is found only in the Galápagos. This bird skims the water for its food. It nests in coastal trees such as mangroves.

Another beautiful native species is the magnificent frigate bird. During its mating season, the male puffs up a red pouch in his chest. The bright color helps attract a mate.

Three-fourths of the world's population of blue-footed boobies lives in the Galápagos Islands.

After their discovery, no one claimed the Galápagos Islands for almost 300 years. Then in 1832, Ecuador took possession of the islands.

For many years, few people went to the Galápagos. Then in 1969, the first tour boat arrived. Today, more than 100,000 tourists visit the islands each year.

The rise in tourism has created problems. Over time, people have brought new plants and animals to the islands. Many threaten the survival of native and endemic species.

Tourists may accidentally bring seeds or tiny insects with them. New plants can take over where native plants grew. And, new insects can bring diseases.

Feral animals can be especially harmful. Wild cats and dogs kill birds and reptiles. Pigs eat bird and tortoise eggs. And, goats take food from native animals.

In 1998, the Special Law for Galápagos was established. It formed a system that limits which species are brought to the islands.

Project Isabela is helping the Galápagos Islands.
This effort works to eliminate wild pigs and goats.

PROTECTING THE ISLANDS

Since the early 1900s, efforts have been made to protect the islands. In 1959, Ecuador founded the Galápagos National Park. It contains 97 percent of the total land.

Then in 1998, the Galápagos Marine Reserve was formed. It protects 53,300 square miles (138,000 sq km) of water and coastline around the islands. Today, the Galápagos National Park Service manages the land and waters of the Galápagos.

Yet, the Galápagos Islands cannot be protected by the park service alone. Scientists at the Charles Darwin Research Station work to better understand the islands. Their research supports the park service's **conservation** efforts.

The Galápagos Islands are home to many rare forms of wildlife. **UNESCO** officials wanted to protect the area. So, they named the Galápagos Islands a World Heritage site in 1978. In 2001, the marine reserve was added to the site.

Even with this protection, the Galápagos Islands still face problems. In 2007, UNESCO officials added the Galápagos to its List of World Heritage in Danger.

Our Valuable World Heritage

Around the globe, UNESCO World Heritage sites represent important civilizations and natural places. Cultural sites include historic buildings, towns, and monuments as well as important archaeological sites. Natural sites contain rare species or natural marvels. Or, they provide important examples of Earth's natural processes. Mixed sites share both cultural and natural elements. World Heritage sites protect and promote these global treasures for future generations.

BALANCING ACT

Many animals in the Galápagos act tame. Still, humans should never touch them.

One of the biggest threats to the Galápagos Islands is people. Fortunately, tourists can help by being friendly to the **environment**. They must not bring any plants or animals onto the islands. Tourists should only look and leave nothing but footprints.

As humans move to the islands, they threaten **natural resources** there. For years, the population grew about 6 percent annually. Then in 2007, Ecuador began working to slow that rate of growth.

Most people in the islands live on San Cristóbal and Santa Cruz.

More than 28,000 people currently call the Galápagos home. They construct buildings and roads on the islands. They plow up native plants to farm the land. Their cars and boats pollute the air and the water.

In addition, many fishermen illegally fish in the protected waters of the Galápagos. This negatively affects marine life around the islands.

Humans need the means to survive on the Galápagos Islands. However, they also need to protect the **environment**. So, educational programs there teach the importance of **conservation**.

Conservationists also promote using clean, renewable energy sources. The Galápagos Energy Blueprint plan works with residents toward this goal.

Now, Floreana islanders use wind and solar energy as power sources. And, Santa Cruz residents recycle much of the oil used by the fishing and tourism industries.

Today, the Galápagos Islands are the best-preserved **archipelago** in the world. And, they are home to many rare and wonderful plants and animals. Humans must work to prevent further harm to these living things. Then, scientists can continue to study the Galápagos. With care, this natural treasure will remain an exciting place for many years.

Galápagos sea lions are a favorite with tourists. Preserving the islands means protecting sea lions and other wonderful animals.

GLOSSARY

archipelago - a group of islands.

conservation - the planned management of rivers, forests, and other natural resources in order to protect and preserve them.

endangered - in danger of becoming extinct.

environment - all the surroundings that affect the growth and well-being of a living thing.

equator - an imaginary circle around the middle of Earth. It is halfway between the North and South poles.

exploit - to make unfair use of.

feral - having gone back to the original wild or untamed state after being tame.

natural resource - a material found in nature that is useful or necessary to life. Water, forests, and minerals are examples of natural resources.

UNESCO - United Nations Educational, Scientific, and Cultural Organization. A special office created by the United Nations in 1945. It aims to promote international cooperation in education, science, and culture.

archipelago - ahr-kuh-PEH-luh-goh
El Niño - ehl NEE-nyoh
Española - ehs-pah-NYOH-lah
feral - FIHR-uhl
Fernandina - fehr-nahn-DEE-nah
flightless cormorant - FLITE-luhs KAWRM-ruhnt
Galápagos Islands - guh-LAH-puh-guhs EYE-luhndz
Isabela - ee-sah-BAY-lah
magnificent frigate bird - mag-NIH-fuh-suhnt FRIH-guht BUHRD
Nazca Plate - NAHS-kah PLAYT
opuntia cactus - oh-PUHNT-shee-uh KAK-tuhs

WEB SITES

To learn more about the Galápagos Islands, visit
ABDO Publishing Company online. Web sites about the Galápagos
Islands are featured on our Book Links page. These links are routinely
monitored and updated to provide the most current information available.
www.abdopublishing.com

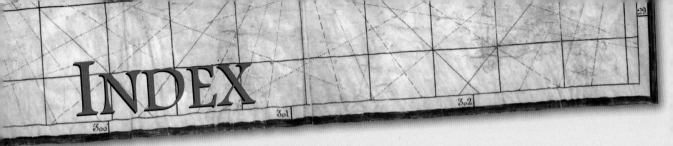

Index